FACTS ABOUT ME

- **My name is** _____
- **I was born in**_____
- **I now live in** _____ , **Colorado.**
- **I have lived in Colorado for** _____ **years.**
- **My birthday is**_____
- **The name of my school is**_____
- **I am in grade** _____
- **My teacher is** _____

Things I like about Colorado:

_____

_____

_____

_____

_____

_____

_____

_____

_____

_____

_____

_____

Some of my favorite places in Colorado:_____

_____

_____

_____

Places I have lived in Colorado:

_____

_____

_____

Places in Colorado I would like to visit:

_____

_____

_____

MY COLORADO

One of the most noticeable things about Colorado is the land. It is a land of great variety. It includes all of the following:

snow-capped peaks	pine forests
deep canyons	flat-topped mesas
white water rivers	aspen groves
grassy meadows	buttes
sand dunes	blue lakes
rolling prairies	plateaus

Which of these do you see in the area where you live? Circle all the terms that apply. Are there other land features in the area where you live? If so, name them.

_____

_____

_____

_____

The name *Colorado* comes from Spanish words meaning "colored red" or "ruddy." The name was first given to the Colorado River because the silt in the river made it look red. Later the name of the land surrounding the Colorado River also became known as "Colorado."

Many other places in Colorado have names that come from Spanish words. *La Junta* and *Buena Vista* are just two of them. Find five towns or cities with Spanish names and place them on the map, right. For help, you might consult an atlas, your parents, your teacher, the Internet or other sources.

One nickname for Colorado is the "Centennial State." *Centennial* means "100th anniversary." Colorado became a state in 1876, during the 100th anniversary of the Declaration of Independence.

Another nickname for Colorado is "Colorful Colorado." Our state is known for its beautiful scenery — the snow-capped mountains, the clear blue skies and the pink, orange and golden sunsets.

Make the border on pages 2 and 3 a "Colorful Colorado" border.

On the █
put a s
where yo

Mark the ma
with differen
to indicate:

1. Where you
   lived ◆
2. Where you
   visited ▲
3. Where you
   like to visit

Describe your community's location in the state as clearly as you can. Do you live o eastern plains? In the Rocky Mountains? In a valley? On the Western Slope? Near Explain.

_____

_____

_____

_____

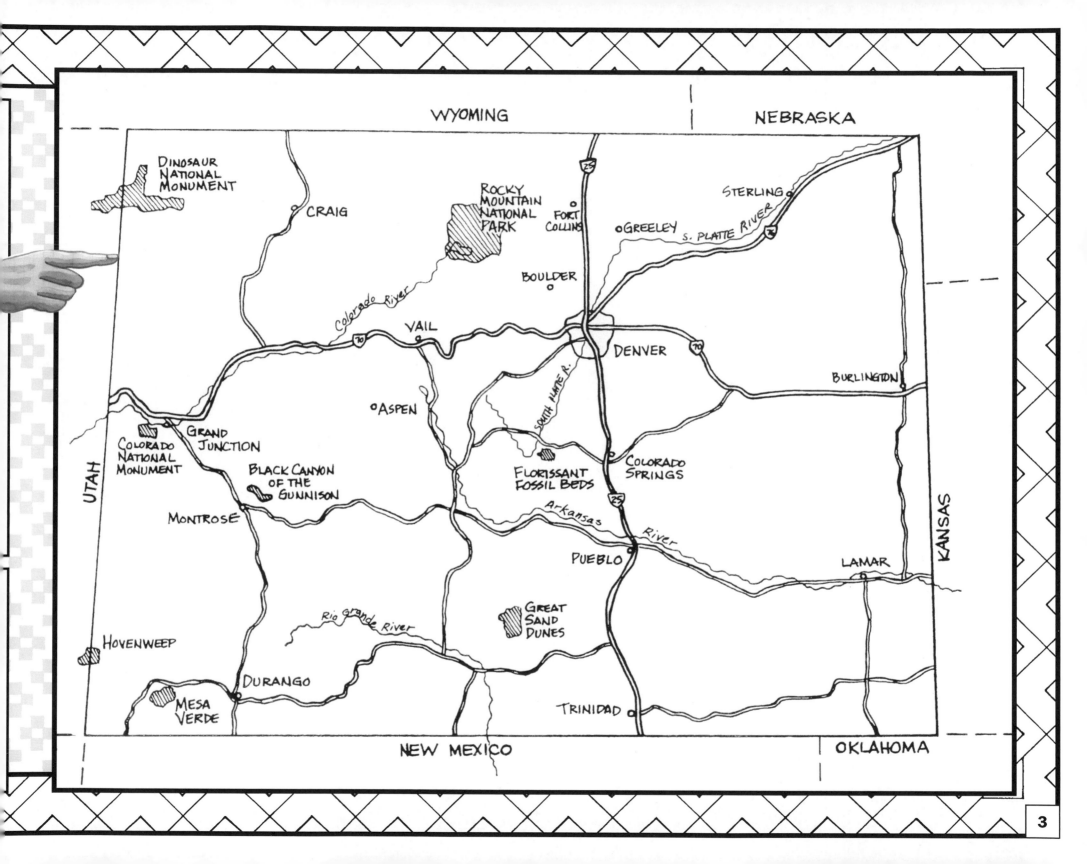

WYOMING

NEBRASKA

DINOSAUR NATIONAL MONUMENT

CRAIG

ROCKY MOUNTAIN NATIONAL PARK

FORT COLLINS

GREELEY

STERLING

S. PLATTE RIVER

BOULDER

Colorado River

VAIL

DENVER

BURLINGTON

ASPEN

SOUTH PLATTE R.

COLORADO NATIONAL MONUMENT

GRAND JUNCTION

FLORISSANT FOSSIL BEDS

COLORADO SPRINGS

BLACK CANYON OF THE GUNNISON

MONTROSE

Arkansas

River

UTAH

PUEBLO

LAMAR

KANSAS

Rio Grande River

GREAT SAND DUNES

HOVENWEEP

DURANGO

MESA VERDE

TRINIDAD

NEW MEXICO

OKLAHOMA

COLORADO AND THE WORLD

Look at a globe in your classroom.

- What latitude does Colorado lie on? _____
- Find 5 cities or countries around the world near the same latitude. List these places bel◄

_____ _____ _____ _____ _____

- How would you expect these places to be similar to Colorado? _____

_____

COLORADO AND THE UNITED STATES

Study the map of the continental United States, right. Label the following:

Colorado

Atlantic Ocean

Canada

Pacific Ocean

Mexico

Gulf of Mexico

Look at the map of the United States, right.

- Color the state of Colorado yellow.

- A coastal state is located next to an ocean. A continental state is located in the interior of a continent, away fro◄ coasts. Is Colorado a coastal state or a continental state? _____

- Which ocean is nearest to the state of Colorado? _____

- Does Colorado lie in the eastern or the western part of the United States? _____

- Two countries border the United States. What are they? _____

  Which one is closest to Colorado? _____

- How do you think being close to this country might have influenced Colorado? _____

  _____

- Which states on the map are bigger than Colorado? _____

  _____ _____ _____ _____

- What states in the continental United States have you visited? Lightly shade these states in the color of your choice, and ◄

A LAND OF GREAT VARIETY

The word "geography" refers to the study of the surface of the earth. It includes looking at the physical features of the land and the division of the earth into continents and countries. It includes the study of climate, plants, animals, natural resources and the people who live in the different areas of the earth.

Geography has a big effect on people's lives. It helps determine what they do, how they live, how they work and how they play. For example, the cold climate of northern Canada means that people who live there wear lots of warm clothing. They may choose skiing instead of scuba diving for a sport.

Think of two more examples of how geography affects the lives of people across the world.

1. _____

_____

_____

2. _____

_____

_____

What If?

Colorado is known to have a fairly dry climate when compared to the rest of the world. What if Colorado were in a rainforest? How would life be different for people living in the state? List at least three ways.

1. _____

_____

_____

2. _____

_____

3. _____

The land of Colorado has always shaped the lives of the humans who have lived here. To understand the history of Colorado and its people, we must first look at the land.

Colorado has three main geographic areas:

plains

plateaus

mountains

On the next pages, you will be exploring all three geographic areas and how they affect the lives of people who live and have lived in Colorado.

How does geography affect your life? Give three examples.

1. _____

_____

_____

2. _____

_____

3. _____

Geography inspires a song

Over 100 years ago, in 1893, a woman from Massachusetts came to Colorado. Katharine Lee Bates, a professor of English literature at Wellesley College, came to spend the summer as a visiting professor at Colorado College in Colorado Springs.

One beautiful summer day, Bates made a trip to the top of Pikes Peak. It is said that her first words upon reaching the summit were "Beautiful!" and "What spacious skies!" In front of her, she could see miles and miles of plains planted in wheat, stretching out to the east for as far as her eyes could see. Behind her she saw the towering, majestic Rocky Mountains extending to the north, west and south.

The geography of the state inspired Katharine Bates to write a poem you have probably heard many times. It begins like this:

O beautiful for spacious skies,
For amber waves of grain,
For purple mountain majesties
Above the fruited plain!
America! America! God shed his grace on thee.
And crown thy good with brotherhood
From sea to shining sea!

The poem is better known as the words to a song. What is the name of the song?

_____

THE GREAT PLAINS

The area of our country known as the Great Plains stretches over parts of ten states. It takes up about a third of all the land in the United States. The land in this area is also sometimes called *prairie* or *grasslands*.

The Great Plains area was created by thousands of feet of dirt and rock being washed down from the Rocky Mountains over hundreds of thousands of years. The dirt and rock that washed down is called *sediment*. In some places, the sediment on the Great Plains is up to four miles thick.

When people first settled east of the Mississippi River in the 1830s and 1840s, they built log houses, like the one Abraham Lincoln lived in as a boy. However, when people later came to settle in Colorado, they couldn't build log houses because there were almost no trees on the plains of Colorado.

The only material available for houses was sod — the grass and soil that covered the plains. The pioneers cut chunks of dirt with the prairie grass still growing in them. They used these chunks to build homes. The homes may not have been beautiful, but they were warm in the winter and cool in the summer. The pioneers called them *soddies*.

Grass on the Great Plains

The grass on the Great Plains is called buffalo grass. It is very tough. It grows only about four to seven inches high, but the roots can grow three to four feet deep or more. The roots of the grass are so long because they are searching for underground pools of water known as *aquifers*. The roots grow tangled and twisted together, making a giant web that holds the soil together and keeps it in place.

What do you think might happen to the topsoil of the Great Plains if the prairie grasses were not there?

_____

_____

_____

_____

_____

Using the description above as a guideline, draw a picture of buffalo grass and its root system below ground.

L

1.

2.

3.

4.

5

...l label Colorado on
...Plains map.

...her Great Plains states.

_____

_____

_____

...other Great Plains states on the map.

...y much of Colorado is a part of the Great
...u can figure this out by dividing Colorado
...qual spaces, using vertical lines. About how
...e fifths make up the Great Plains?)

_____

_____

...ties located on the Great Plains. Then
... on the map, right. Include the capital of

_____   _____

Great Plains

MORE GREAT PLAINS

The Great Plains — In the Past

Grass was the food for the thousands and thousands of buffalo that roamed across the plains of Colorado until the mid to late 1800s. Buffalo herds were very important to the Native American tribes in the area. These Great Plains Indians included the Cheyenne, Arapaho, Sioux, Kiowa, Pawnee and Comanche tribes. They used the buffalo for many basic needs of every day life.

The hide of the buffalo was used to make clothing and shelter. The meat was used for food. That was only the beginning. Buffalo also had many, many more uses. What part of the buffalo might have been used for each of the following:

tools	writing "paper"
utensils	fuel
glue	peace pipes
string	blankets
musical instruments	"moving vans"

When people use the word *plains*, they are referr____ flat. However, the Great Plains aren't really co____ are dips and rises in the land, as well as small hills a____ valleys. The Great Plains appear flat when we look ou____ a distance. Also, compared to the Rocky Mountains r____ them, they look very flat indeed!

1. The area of the Great Plains close to the Rocky M____ is commonly called the *Front Range*. Why do you____ Front Range? _____
_____

2. Eighty percent of Colorado's population lives alon____ Why do you think this is true? _____
_____

3. Interstate 25 connects the cities of the Front Rang____ map, right, locate Interstate 25 and color it purple____

4. Locate the following Front Range cities and circle____ green.

    Fort Collins   *Pueblo*

    Denver   *Trinidad*

5. Most of the towns on the eastern plains of Colora____ Front Range cities and towns. Most of them have____ What does *agricultural* mean?_____

6. Find each of the following towns on the eastern p____ highlight each in yellow.

    Sterling   *Burlington*

7. Using another Colorado map for help, place each____ towns of the eastern plains on the map, right:

    Fort Morgan   *La Junta*

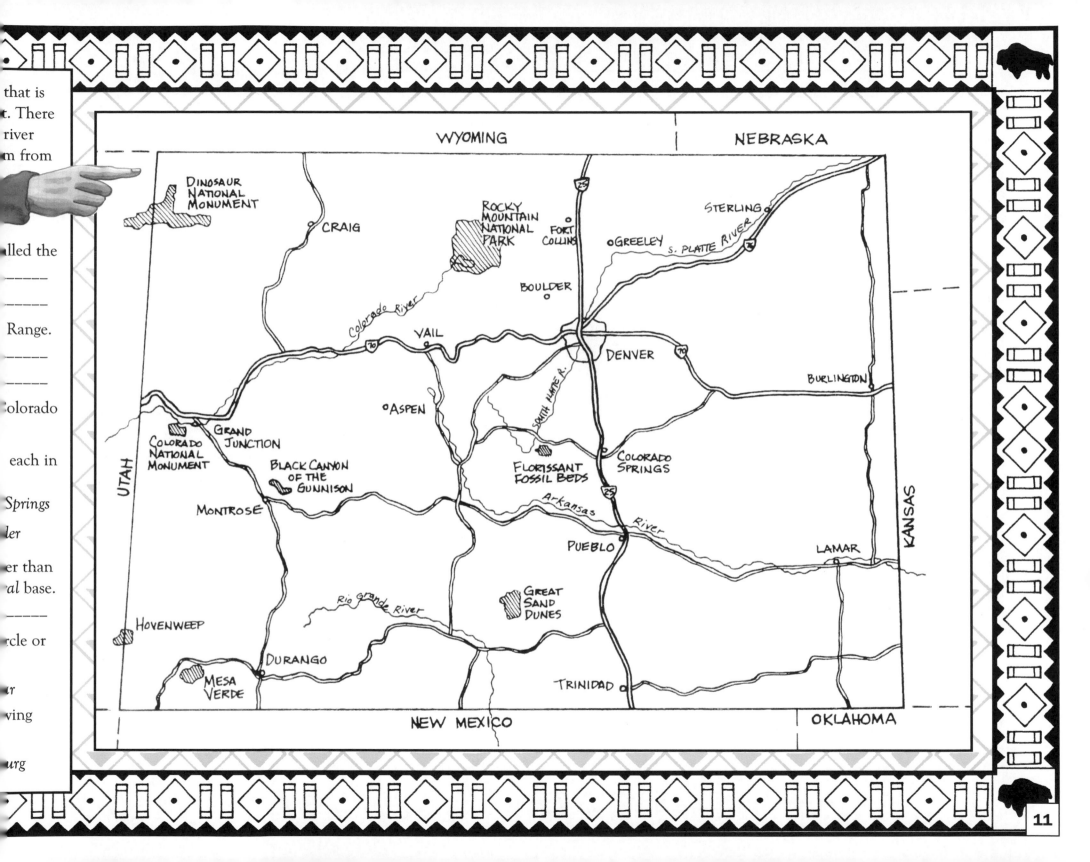

that is
t. There
river
m from

lled the

_____

Range.

_____

_____

Colorado

_____

each in

_____

Springs

ler

er than

al base.

_____

rcle or

ur

ving

urg

WYOMING

NEBRASKA

DINOSAUR NATIONAL MONUMENT

CRAIG

ROCKY MOUNTAIN NATIONAL PARK

STERLING

FORT COLLINS

GREELEY

S. PLATTE RIVER

BOULDER

Colorado River

VAIL

DENVER

BURLINGTON

ASPEN

SOUTH PLATTE R.

COLORADO NATIONAL MONUMENT

GRAND JUNCTION

BLACK CANYON OF THE GUNNISON

FLORISSANT FOSSIL BEDS

COLORADO SPRINGS

MONTROSE

Arkansas River

PUEBLO

LAMAR

UTAH

Rio Grande River

GREAT SAND DUNES

KANSAS

HOVENWEEP

DURANGO

MESA VERDE

TRINIDAD

NEW MEXICO

OKLAHOMA

Look at the map of Colorado, right.

1. About how much of Colorado includes the Rocky Mountains? (You can figure this out by dividing Colorado into five equal spaces, using vertical lines. About how many of the fifths make up the Rocky Mountains?) _____

2. Sometimes Colorado is considered a Great Plains state. Other times, it is considered a Rocky Mountain state. If you had to choose, which label do you think fits Colorado best? Why? _____

_____

3. A single mountain is sometimes called a peak. You may have heard of Longs Peak and Pikes Peak. Mark the location of these peaks on the map at right and color them red.

4. A group of connected mountains is called a range. Colorado has several mountain ranges. On the map, right, color each of the ranges a different color.

5. What two mountain ranges form a wall that faces out toward the Great Plains?

_____

6. What are the names of the two southern mountain ranges?

_____

These names tell you something about early settlers to this region. Who do you think they were?_____

7. Locate and label the town or city where you live. Which mountain range is closest to you?

_____

8. Running along the top of the Rocky Mountains is the Continental Divide, which separates the Colorado Rockies into two sections known as the Western Slope and the Eastern Slope. Find the Continental Divide on your map. Color it dark brown or black. Which side of the Continental Divide do you live on? _____

9. The Continental Divide divides the way water flows in America. On the west side of the Divide, it flows to the west. On the east side, it flows to the east. Draw arrows pointing east on the eastern side of the Continental Divide. Draw arrows pointing west on the western side of the Continental Divide.

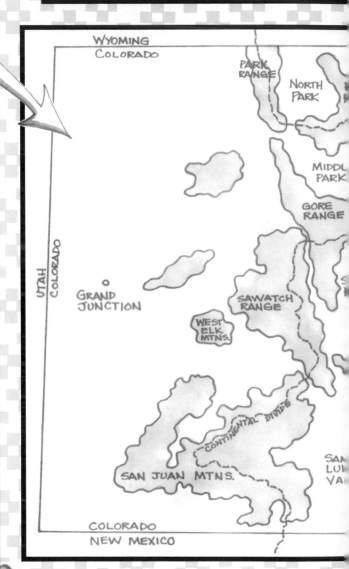

UNTAINS

Colorado Mountain Ranges and Parks

o DENVER

o PUEBLO

COLORADO
KANSAS

What is a "fourteener"? Close to the Continental Divide are 54 mountains that rise 14,000 feet or higher above sea level. These mountains provide a special challenge to mountain climbers from all over the world. Once a person has climbed all 54 "fourteeners," he or she is said to become a member of the "Fourteeners Club."

Find the names of six 14,000 foot "cloud scrapers." List them below. Then locate each on your map, left, by drawing a black cone.

_____   _____   _____

_____   _____   _____

What is a park? A mountain park is a large, open, flat expanse of land located at a high altitude and ringed by mountains. Look at the four mountain parks on the map, left. Three of the parks are nearly treeless regions of green grass. The fourth park is so dry it is nearly a desert.

- On your map, locate North Park, home to many deer, antelope, elk and newly introduced moose. Shade it light green.
- Locate Middle Park, location of the headwaters of the Colorado River. Shade it light blue.
- Locate South Park, one of the places where gold was discovered in 1859. Shade it light orange.
- Locate the San Luis Valley, which is commonly called a "valley" but really is a park. It is a very dry area where the Great Sand Dunes National Park is located. Shade it light brown.

What is a glacier? Most people think of places like Antarctica when they think of glaciers. However, you can also find glaciers in Colorado. A glacier is a large, permanent mass of ice that moves very slowly. It is created when more snow falls during the winter than melts in the summer. Over many years, the fallen snow compresses into ice. St. Mary's Glacier is near Idaho Springs. There are also several glaciers in Rocky Mountain National Park.

Hot Springs

More than 90 large geothermal hot springs are located in the Rocky Mountains. Hot springs are areas where hot or warm groundwater comes out of the ground. They are created when cold water, often from snow melt, trickles down thousands of feet through cracks in the earth to the hot rocks at the center of the earth. There the water heats up. Because heat rises, the water moves through other cracks back up to the earth's surface and bubbles out into hot springs.

For centuries, hot springs were sacred, spiritual places to the Utes, who lived high in the Rocky Mountains. The Utes held ceremonies and rituals at many hot springs.

In the past, many people moved to Colorado because they believed the minerals in waters from hot springs cured arthritis, cancer, epilepsy, tuberculosis and many other ailments. Some Colorado hot springs became so popular for healing and bathing that the communities were named after the springs. The best known are Glenwood Springs, Hot Sulphur Springs, Manitou Springs, Steamboat Springs, Idaho Springs and Pagosa Springs.

Bubbly water. The springs at Manitou Springs pass through rock that contains carbon. The water picks up carbonic acid, making carbonated water — just like the fizzy ingredient in carbonated soft drinks.

Chugging water. The springs at Steamboat Springs used to make a chugging noise that reminded early settlers of a Mississippi River steamboat. That's how Steamboat Springs got its name!

Mountain Men: Trappers of the West

In the 1820s and 1830s, many men wore hats made from beaver fur. Because beavers lived along all the rivers in the area that later became Colorado, trappers soon came to trap the beavers and take their pelts. Pelts are the hide of the animal with the fur still on it.

The trappers learned all the trails and routes through the mountains and on the plains. They came west in large groups, but when they got to the Rocky Mountains, they separated and trapped by themselves. It was a lonely existence for most of the year, but once or twice a year these trappers or "mountain men" gathered together to trade pelts for clothing, tools, gunpowder and new traps. Because the very first trappers were French, these meetings were called *rendezvous*, the French word for gathering.

ROCKY M

The Rocky Mountains presented travelers in the early days of Co mountains to get to what they nee best ways to pass through the mou pass through, they called them *pas*

Travelers sometimes named a p Ears Pass near Steamboat Springs named a pass after their home stat they named a pass for a famous pe man David H. Moffat. Loveland Pa Loveland. Some other passes in Co Cottonwood Pass, Half Moon Pass Creek Pass, La Veta Pass, Los Piño

1. What would you expect to see a

_____

2. What would you expect to find

_____

3. Choose one mountain pass. If pass, what would you name it?

_____

_____

_____

n for miners, trappers and other
ow could they travel over the
other side? They had to find the
en they discovered these places to
e them names.

at they saw in the rocks. Rabbit
ple. Sometimes the travelers
mple, Tennessee Pass. Sometimes
at Pass is named after railroad
d after railroad man William A.
Cochetopa Pass, Cinnamon Pass,
ence Pass, Tincup Pass, Trout
Mosquito Pass.

ead Pass? _____

_____

nwood Pass? _____

_____

mountain man discovering this

_____

_____

_____

Mining

Gold and silver. Mining in Colorado began with the discovery of gold in 1859 along Little Dry Creek near Denver. William Green Russell and a small band of prospectors from Georgia found placer gold in the stream. Placer gold is gold flakes that have rubbed off larger nuggets.

News of gold in Colorado started a rush that brought thousands of people, mostly men, in search of riches. These prospectors flocked to the streams flowing out of the mountains, hoping to get rich quickly. However, they soon found that there wasn't much gold just lying around waiting for them. They had to dig deep into the mountains in search of riches. Mining was very hard work, and few prospectors made much money at it.

When the miners came to Colorado, there weren't any towns, so they started their own. Sometimes gold miners named the towns they started for their location, like Central City. Sometimes they named the towns for what they found there. For example, Placerville was named for placer gold. Sometimes they named them for what they hoped to have happen there — Fairplay, for example.

In the 1870s, the discovery of silver in Colorado started another "Rush to the Rockies." Silverton, Silver Cliff and La Plata (Spanish for *silver*) were all towns that were founded during the silver boom.

Many towns that were founded during the gold and silver rushes are abandoned now. We call them ghost towns because all that is left are the empty buildings and silent streets.

Coal. At the turn of the century coal was needed to heat homes and provide power for steam engines and factories. Great beds of coal lay in southern Colorado around Trinidad, and new towns grew up around the coal mines. Two of them were La Veta (Spanish for *the vein*), and Boncarbo, from the French words *bon charbon*, meaning "good coal."

Miners worked long hours, thousands of feet underground in the freezing cold. There was always the danger that the earth would cave in on them or that gas from the newly mined coal would poison them. The miners used dynamite to blast out the coal, but it often misfired, bringing the supporting timbers crashing down. Because miners breathed in coal dust year after year, they often developed a disease called black lung.

If you were coming to Colorado in the 1800s, would you rather have been a miner or a trapper? Why? Explain.

_____

_____

_____

_____

_____

_____

_____

COLORADO PLAT

A plateau is a high area of relatively level land. The Colorado Plateau is really a huge area filled with many plateaus. It covers parts of four states.

The Colorado Plateau is over 500 million years old. Many, many years ago, warm shallow seas often covered the area. The area would fill up, and then the waters would recede, leaving tons of sediment behind. If you find a sandy place on the Colorado Plateau today and start digging around, you might discover petrified oyster and clam shells left over from ancient times!

Over the years, layer after layer of sediment built up on the Colorado Plateau. The layers gradually sank under their own weight. Heat and pressure hardened the sediment into rock several miles thick.

At the same time that the layers of sediment were being laid down, volcanoes were erupting. Sometimes lava flowed over the surface of the earth. Sometimes liquid rock called magma could not reach the surface because of the hard layer of rock. The land was pushed upward, forming mountain ranges, including the Rocky Mountains.

1. On the map at right, color the area inside the dotted lines yellow. This is the Colorado Plateau.

2. What four states are included in the Colorado Plateau?

   _____ _____ _____ _____

   Label these states on the map.

3. Outline Colorado in red.

4. About how much of Colorado is a part of the Colorado Plateau? (*Again, you can figure this out by dividing Colorado into five equal spaces, using ver how many fifths include the Colorado Plateau?*) _____

5. On the map, find the two Colorado cities located on the Colorado Plateau. Ci them in green.

6. Make a blue circle around the Four Corners area. This place is the only place i United States where you can be in four states at the same time! How is this po what you would have to do.

   _____

   _____

   _____

   _____

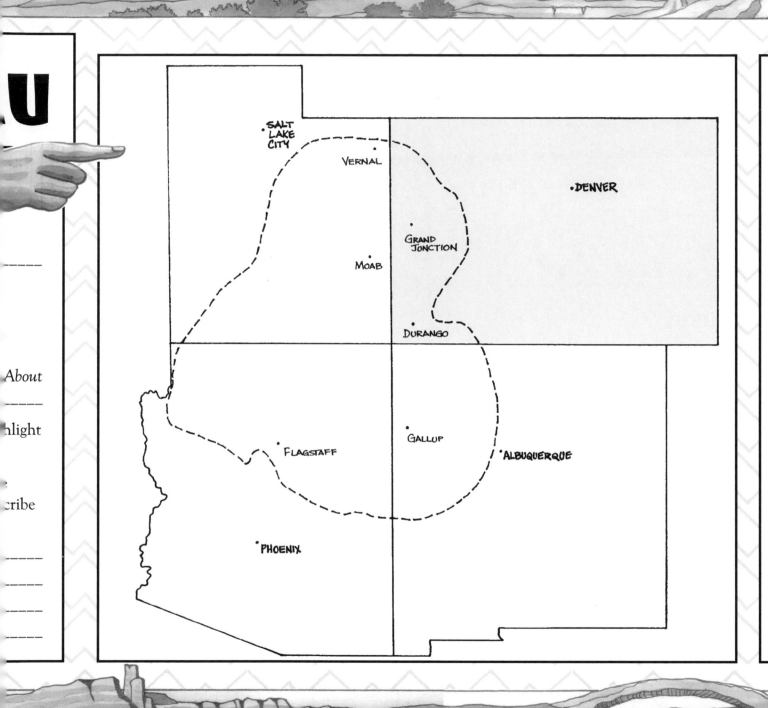

U

About

hlight

cribe

Did You Know?

There is a story that one cold night about 130 years ago, a group of tired travelers built a campfire. They built it against a wall of rocks so that the nearby grasses would not catch fire.

Suddenly the rocks caught fire! That is because the rocks were oil shale. Oil shale is a rock that contains material that can be heated to produce oil. The Colorado Plateau is very rich in oil shale, but it is very difficult and very costly to mine the oil shale and produce the oil. Therefore, the oil shale sits, unused.

Ancestral Puebloans (sometimes called the Anasazi) moved into the canyons of the Colorado Plateau in about 1000 A.D. There they built complex structures out of adobe and quarried stone. They built homes and grain storage areas. They dug large ceremonial places called *kivas*. We know this area today as Mesa Verde.

The Ancestral Puebloans chose the Mesa Verde area because it provided three things they needed:

- **Water.** Water was trapped in the layers of rock along the canyon walls.

- **Food.** Turkeys, rabbits and deer provided meat. Trees and shrubs at the top of the canyons provided roots and berries.

- **Protection.** The steep canyons protected the people from harsh weather and enemies.

When the water dried up and the animals went away, the people had to move, too. Today the ruins of their buildings show us where they lived.

Erosion created many rock formations on the Colorado Pla
often by wind blowing and beating on rocks or water rushi
following rock formations created by erosion.

mesa: a high, flat-topped mountain with steep sides. It is wider than it is high. Mesa means *table* in Spanish.

butte: a smal
a flat top and
alone.

canyon: a deep valley with steep s
eroded by water.

on refers to the slow and gradual changing of landforms,
ng through rock and soil. Draw a picture of each of the

untain with
standing

spire: a tall narrow piece of land carved by erosion and coming to a point at the top.

: a curved rock formation that
mbles a bridge.

Rock Art

People from early civilizations wrote the stories of their lives in carvings and pictures they left on stone canyon walls, not only on the Colorado Plateau, but also throughout southern Colorado. Their ancient "books" help us understand how the people lived and worked together.

A *pictograph* is a picture used to tell about an event or an idea. When a picture is carved into rock, it is called a *petroglyph*.

A pictograph for "person" might look like this:

A pictograph for "buffalo" might look like this:

A pictograph for "deer" might look like this:

Invent some pictographs of your own. Use the boxes below to "tell" about something in your life today. Be sure your pictographs are ones that other people will be likely to understand.

CLIMATE & PRECIPITATION

Let it snow, let it snow, let it snow!

Colorado's mountains receive a great deal of snow in an average winter. On Wolf Creek Pass in southern Colorado, the average annual snowfall is 465 inches!

Kinds of snow. Some snow is moist, easily packed and great for making snowballs. Some snow is dry, light and powdery. It is terrible for making snowballs, but skiers love it. Ten inches of fresh snow can contain anywhere from a tenth of an inch of water to as much as four inches of water.

All this snow is important for several reasons. For one thing, the ski industry depends on snow for its success in winter. All snow provides greatly needed moisture for Colorado when it melts in the spring and summer. Name at least one industry that depends on moisture from melted snow in the summertime. _____

Problems with snow. One problem that results from a lot of snow is the threat of avalanches. *Avalanche* is a French word that means "slipping down." An avalanche occurs when a large amount of snow suddenly and quickly slides down a mountain with a great roar. As it slides, it often gets bigger and bigger, picking up more and more snow, earth and rock as it goes. An avalanche is very dangerous because it swallows up everything in its path. It can bury skiers, people on snowmobiles, people in cars and others under tons of snow. Luckily, experts in the mountains can usually tell when and where avalanches may occur. Often, they can prevent them, using explosives to create controlled snow slides.

Another problem with snow is blizzards. A blizzard is a severe storm with so much falling and blowing snow that it is difficult to see. A blizzard can create many problems for people and animals alike. List at least five problems that can result from a blizzard in the area where you live:

1._____

2._____

3._____

4._____

5._____

Colorado Precipitation

Precipitation is the amount of rain, snow, sleet or any other form of water that is deposited in an area. Study the map, right, which shows Colorado's average annual precipitation.

1. How much precipitation does most of Colorado receive in a year, on the average? _____

_____

2. Which parts of Colorado receive the highest amount of precipitation?

_____

3. Which part receives the lowest amount? _____

Annual Precipitation Map of Colorado

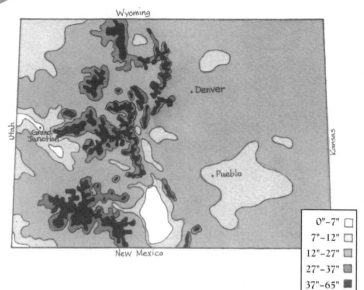

Legend	
0"–7"	☐
7"–12"	☐
12"–27"	▨
27"–37"	▨
37"–65"	■

Annual Precipitation Map of North America

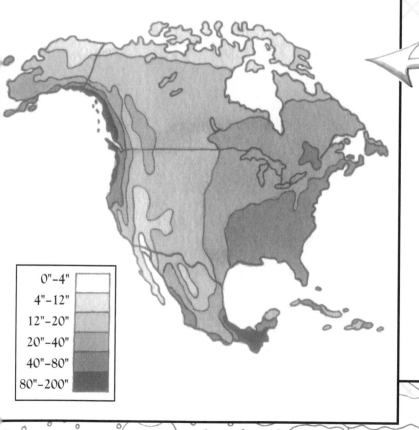

Legend	
0"–4"	
4"–12"	
12"–20"	
20"–40"	
40"–80"	
80"–200"	

North American Precipitation

Now study the map that shows the annual precipitation of North America.

1. How does Colorado's climate compare with other areas of North America?

_____

_____

_____

2. Is Colorado's precipitation typical of the western United States? Explain.

_____

_____

_____

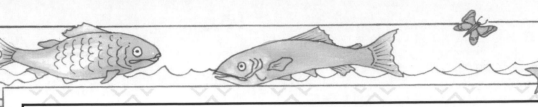

Rivers

1. There are four important river systems that start in Colorado and connect our state to the rest of the United States. Find these rivers on the map, right. Color them blue.

Colorado River:

It links Colorado to the West Coast, ending in the Gulf of California.

Rio Grande

It connects southern Colorado with the Southwest.

Arkansas River & South Platte River

They connect eastern Colorado to the other Great Plains states.

2. Colorado's four important river systems also have very important *tributaries*. Tributaries are rivers that join and "contribute" to the flow of a major river. Four Colorado tributaries are listed below. Find these rivers on the map and color them red.

Purgatoire River   **Gunnison River**

Cache la Poudre River   **Conejos River**

3. Find the Continental Divide on the map. Color it green.

4. The beginnings of rivers are called the *headwaters*. If all water flows downhill, then where are the headwaters of Colorado's rivers located? _____

Did You Know?

Farmers sometimes use huge sprinklers to irrigate their fields. Pipes attach these sprinklers to wells. Because these sprinklers are on wheels and rotate around the well pump, they are called center pivot irrigation systems. If you travel across the Great Plains in an airplaine, you can look down and see the giant circles of green crops created by center pivot irrigation.

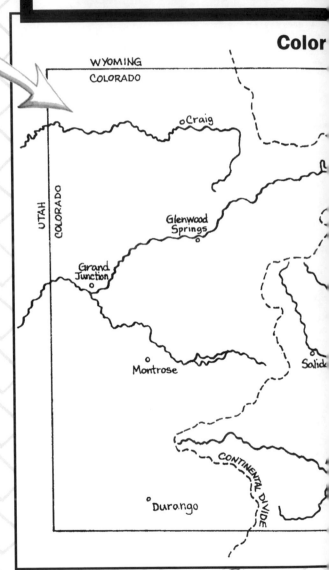

RIVERS

Color

WYOMING
COLORADO

UTAH
COLORADO

oCraig

Glenwood Springs

Grand Junction

Montrose

Salida

CONTINENTAL DIVIDE

oDurango

WATER

ivers

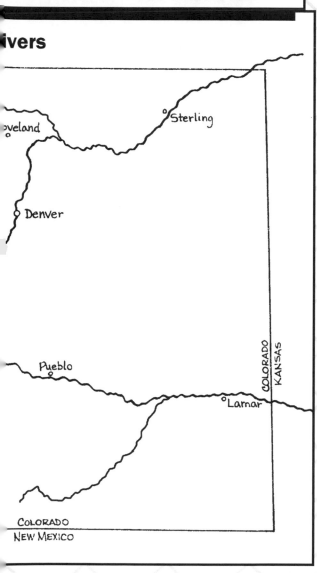

Colorado Water Sources and Rights

As you have already learned, Colorado receives an average of only 10 to 15 inches of moisture a year. That is not enough to grow crops or keep lawns green in the summer.

The people of eastern Colorado have solved the problem of lack of moisture in two ways:

- Thousands of miles of ditches and canals bring water from the South Platte, Rio Grande and Arkansas Rivers to fields where water is needed for crops.

- Deep, deep wells reach down to the aquifer for water. The aquifer is an underground layer of rock and sand that contains water. People pump the water out of the aquifer and use it for drinking, washing and irrigating crops.

The Front Range area of Colorado has a huge need for water because of the large number of people living there. The area gets much of its water from the Colorado River.

How can that be? As you have seen, the Colorado River is on the western side of the Continental Divide and flows west. The Front Range is on the eastern side of the mountains. How does the Colorado River end up coming out of faucets in Fort Collins, Greeley, Denver and Pueblo?

The answer is reservoirs and pipes. Water from the Western Slope is saved in huge reservoirs like Shadow Mountain Reservoir, Lake Granby and Lake Dillon. The water is then piped over and through the Continental Divide for use by people along the Front Range.

Precious water. Water is precious in Colorado. It also is the cause of many disagreements and lawsuits. Is it fair to take water from one part of the state for use by another? Is it fair *not* to divert the water if people elsewhere need it? These are questions that people have a hard time settling throughout the western United States. As the population continues to grow, the problems of water and water rights will also continue to grow.

ANIMALS of COLORADO

The **bighorn sheep** is the state animal of Colorado. It is found high in the Rocky Mountains. Bighorn sheep can climb nearly straight up the face of granite rock. Their hooves are shaped to find and fit into the cracks and crevices on the mountainside.

Elk also live in the high country. The elk is a member of the deer family, but it is much larger than a deer. The male elk, called a "bull," grows a huge set of spreading antlers each year. As the elk ages, each new set of antlers is larger than the last and has more "points."

White-tailed deer and **mule deer** live in Colorado, too. These gentle creatures eat green plants and other vegetation. People gave the mule deer its name because of its huge, floppy ears that resemble the ears on the mules the pioneers used to pull their wagons west.

Black bears grow to be very large — an average of 175 pounds for females and 275 pounds for males. They are *reclusive*. That means they like to be left alone. They eat mostly berries and fish, but they will eat other small mammals, too.

Prairie dogs are not really dogs at all. They are rodents, like mice or rats. Prairie dogs live near each other in big colonies that people often call prairie dog towns.

Jack rabbits are native to the Colorado plains and plateau regions. They have big hind feet that help them run fast and change direction very quickly. They also have big, long ears that allow them to capture sounds from a long distance.

Coyotes roam all over Colorado. A coyote is a small wolf-like animal that eats mice, rabbits and other small animals. Coyotes are quick and smart. They "talk" to each other by barking in a high, shrill manner. They make such a racket that people who haven't heard the sound before are often frightened by it.

Colorado is famous for the **trout** that live in its lakes, rivers and streams. In the sunlight, the **rainbow trout** looks like it has multi-colored scales. The **brown trout** has brown speckles or freckles on its back. The **cutthroat trout** has bright red gills that make it look like it is bleeding from its throat.

1. How many of the animals included: beaver, bighorn s fox, garter snake, jack rabbi sel, white-tailed deer.

2. Put a star beside all the an

Many more animals live in land, for example, live fo **beavers, bobcats** and **weasels.** I **walleye pike, catfish, bluegill** a

Choose one animal that described on these pages, and about it. Summarize what you

_____

_____

_____

_____

_____

_____

_____

these pages can you name? Write the names beside the pictures. Here are the animals
bear, bluegill, bobcat, brown trout, bull snake, catfish, coyote, crappie, cutthroat trout, elk,
r, muskrat, prairie dog, rainbow trout, rattlesnake, smallmouth bass, walleye pike, wea-

ive in your area of Colorado.

Reptiles. Millions of years ago, the largest reptile of all time roamed
Colorado. It was, of course, the dinosaur. Many kinds of dinosaurs lived
here, including the brontosaurus, the stegosaurus, and tyrannosaurus. Colorado
even has an official state fossil — the stegosaurus.

Today, Colorado's reptiles are much smaller than the dinosaur. The most com-
mon are **lizards**, **snakes**, **toads** and **frogs**. One kind of snake popular with farmers is
the **bull snake**. It is not poisonous and loves to eat mice and other rodents that eat
the corn and wheat farmers store for the winter.

Garter snakes live in gardens and shady places where they can find and eat
insects. Gardeners like garter snakes because they eat the bugs that like to chew up
the plants in backyard gardens. Garter snakes are not poisonous and are usually so
small that they can hide among the leafy vegetables.

The most well-known snake in Colorado is probably the **rattlesnake**. Rattlesnakes
can be deadly. They have a poison called "venom" that can make people very ill or
even cause them to die. When a rattlesnake is startled or afraid, it shakes the rattles
at the end of its tail to warn intruders to leave quickly. If they don't leave, it strikes.

Rattlesnakes are very sociable — at least with other rattlesnakes. They live in
dens, helping to keep each other warm during the winter months. They are cold-
blooded, which means that they cannot produce body heat to keep themselves
warm. They need help from the sun, the warm earth or other rattlesnakes.

Rattlesnake Kate

One day in Weld County in 1925,
a farm woman stopped her horse
to open a fence gate. She saw a
rattlesnake, so she got out her
Remington 22 rifle and shot it.
Suddenly, three more snakes
appeared. She shot them too.
The shots woke a whole den of
rattlesnakes, but by then she was out of
ammunition.

She was on foot near her horse, and
her three-year-old son was in the saddle.
The snakes began to come out of the
ground, one after the other. She couldn't
get to her horse or her son, so she had
to fight off the snakes herself, without
any bullets in her rifle. For the next
three hours she whacked at snakes with
a fence post. When the snakes stopped
coming out of the den, she stopped and
counted the dead ones that surrounded
her. She had killed 140 rattlesnakes!

She skinned the snakes and made
a dress from the skins. From then on,
she was known as "Rattlesnake Kate."
The dress she made can be seen at the
Greeley Municipal Museum.

INSECTS of COLORADO

1. How many of the insects pictured on these pages can you name? Write the names beside the pictures. Here are the insects included: ants, beetle, butterfly, caterpillar, dragonfly, earwig, flea, grasshopper, hairstreak butterfly, honeybee, ladybug, miller moth, mosquito, moth, pill bug, swallowtail butterfly, termite, water strider.

2. Put a star beside all the insects that live in your area of Colorado.

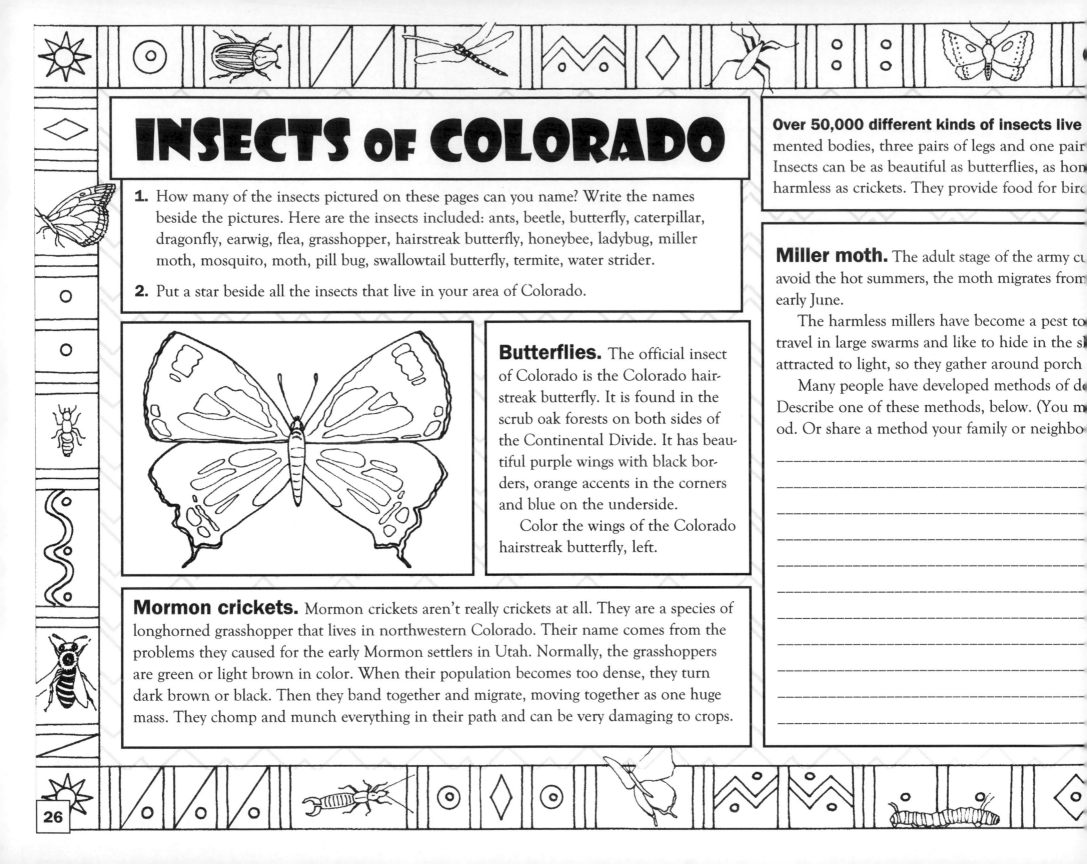

Butterflies. The official insect of Colorado is the Colorado hairstreak butterfly. It is found in the scrub oak forests on both sides of the Continental Divide. It has beautiful purple wings with black borders, orange accents in the corners and blue on the underside.

Color the wings of the Colorado hairstreak butterfly, left.

Mormon crickets. Mormon crickets aren't really crickets at all. They are a species of longhorned grasshopper that lives in northwestern Colorado. Their name comes from the problems they caused for the early Mormon settlers in Utah. Normally, the grasshoppers are green or light brown in color. When their population becomes too dense, they turn dark brown or black. Then they band together and migrate, moving together as one huge mass. They chomp and munch everything in their path and can be very damaging to crops.

Over 50,000 different kinds of insects live mented bodies, three pairs of legs and one pair Insects can be as beautiful as butterflies, as hon harmless as crickets. They provide food for bir

Miller moth. The adult stage of the army cu avoid the hot summers, the moth migrates from early June.

The harmless millers have become a pest to travel in large swarms and like to hide in the s attracted to light, so they gather around porch

Many people have developed methods of de Describe one of these methods, below. (You m od. Or share a method your family or neighbo

_____

_____

_____

_____

_____

_____

_____

_____

_____

Mountain region. Insects have seg-
When they are adults, most have wings.
oppers, as annoying as mosquitoes or as
d some mammals.

---

wn as the "miller" or "miller moth." To
the mountains every year in late May and

ople now living in Colorado. The moths
window sills and doorways. They are
and ceiling lights.

e invasion of miller moths each summer.
ult to describe his or her favorite meth-

Did You Know?

Did you know that a favorite
snack for a grizzly bear is the
miller moth? Although grizzly bears no longer live in
Colorado, they live not far away
in Yellowstone National Park.

Grasshoppers. In the 1930s, swarms of grasshoppers invaded Colorado and caused tre-
mendous damage. A few years ago, a man wrote about the invasion as he remembered it when
he was a boy living on a farm east of Greeley.

*It was pretty bad in the grasshopper days. Grasshoppers would come in clouds and blot out the sun. They
were so thick sometimes that you would look at a fence post and you couldn't see the post — just solid
grasshoppers. It looked like a post of grasshoppers.*

*Every morning we would spread grasshopper poison, which was a bran made up of a poison and
banana oil. There would be a lot of grasshoppers die from that poison. You would see them thick on the
ground, just as thick as could be.*

*We made a grasshopper catcher about 16 feet wide. It was about three or four feet wide at the bottom,
and then it came straight up the back and slanted up. The slanted part was lined with tin. We would put
two horses on the catcher and drive it down the hay field.*

*The grasshoppers would hit the tin, and then they couldn't hang on to it. They would slide down and get
into a slot like a fly catcher in the back end. There was a box back there, and when we got to the end of the
field we would spray the grasshoppers with a kerosene sprayer. They couldn't fly, and it wouldn't be very
long and they would die from the spray.*

*When we got to the end of the field, we would
take a scoop shovel and scoop those grasshoppers
out of there and put them in a pile. I mean, there
were piles three and four feet high, hundreds and
hundreds of pounds of grasshoppers lying on every
end of the field. It smelled pretty bad, too, after a
few days.*

Ivan Klein

Using his description as a guide, draw a picture
or diagram that shows Ivan Klein's method
of catching and killing grasshoppers.

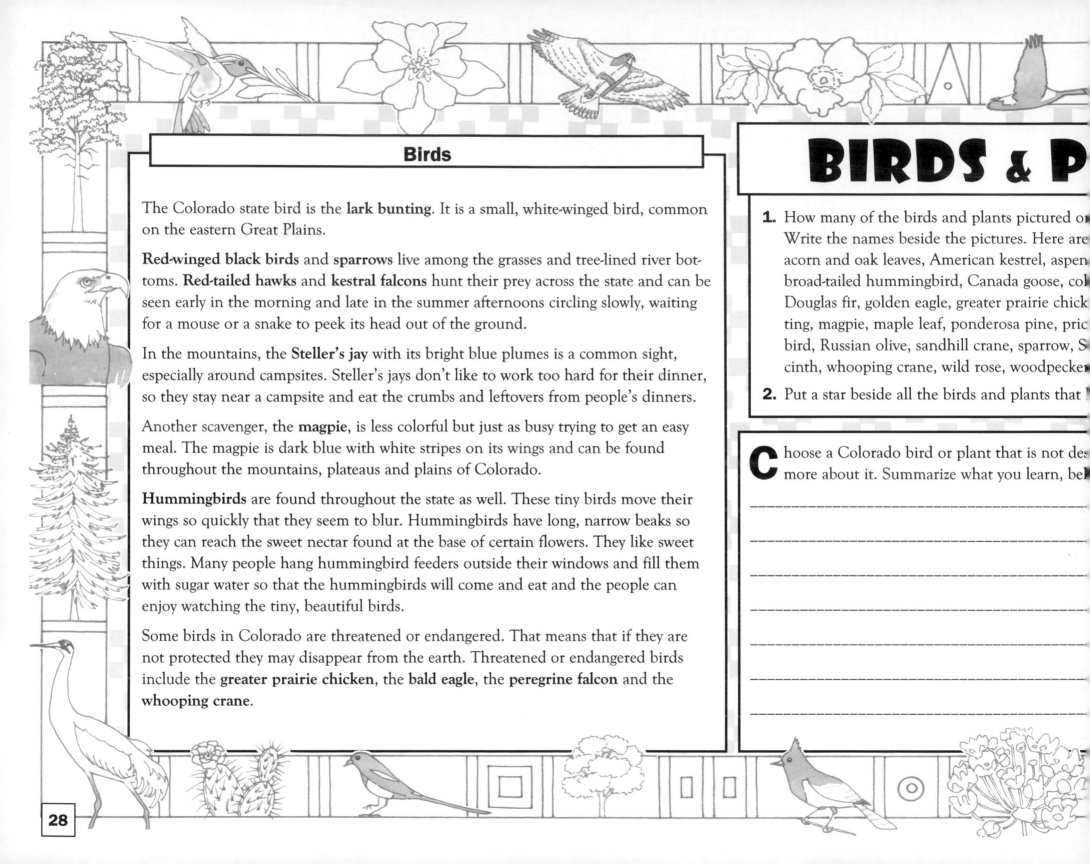

Birds

The Colorado state bird is the **lark bunting**. It is a small, white-winged bird, common on the eastern Great Plains.

Red-winged black birds and **sparrows** live among the grasses and tree-lined river bottoms. **Red-tailed hawks** and **kestral falcons** hunt their prey across the state and can be seen early in the morning and late in the summer afternoons circling slowly, waiting for a mouse or a snake to peek its head out of the ground.

In the mountains, the **Steller's jay** with its bright blue plumes is a common sight, especially around campsites. Steller's jays don't like to work too hard for their dinner, so they stay near a campsite and eat the crumbs and leftovers from people's dinners.

Another scavenger, the **magpie**, is less colorful but just as busy trying to get an easy meal. The magpie is dark blue with white stripes on its wings and can be found throughout the mountains, plateaus and plains of Colorado.

Hummingbirds are found throughout the state as well. These tiny birds move their wings so quickly that they seem to blur. Hummingbirds have long, narrow beaks so they can reach the sweet nectar found at the base of certain flowers. They like sweet things. Many people hang hummingbird feeders outside their windows and fill them with sugar water so that the hummingbirds will come and eat and the people can enjoy watching the tiny, beautiful birds.

Some birds in Colorado are threatened or endangered. That means that if they are not protected they may disappear from the earth. Threatened or endangered birds include the **greater prairie chicken**, the **bald eagle**, the **peregrine falcon** and the **whooping crane**.

BIRDS & P

1. How many of the birds and plants pictured o
   Write the names beside the pictures. Here are
   acorn and oak leaves, American kestrel, aspen
   broad-tailed hummingbird, Canada goose, co
   Douglas fir, golden eagle, greater prairie chick
   ting, magpie, maple leaf, ponderosa pine, pric
   bird, Russian olive, sandhill crane, sparrow, S
   cinth, whooping crane, wild rose, woodpecke

2. Put a star beside all the birds and plants that

Choose a Colorado bird or plant that is not des
more about it. Summarize what you learn, be

_____

_____

_____

_____

_____

_____

_____

Plants

Colorado's millions of acres of forest land contain **spruce, aspen, fir** and **pine trees**. On the Great Plains, **cottonwood** trees grow along the rivers, and **grasses** cover the uncultivated land. The Colorado Plateau contains acres of **sage brush, scrub oak** and **serviceberry shrubs**.

There are many very high places in Colorado where the environment is so harsh, so cold and so rocky that trees cannot grow. Look at the top of any high mountain (or at a picture of one). The line where the trees stop is the *timberline*. The country above timberline is called the *tundra*. The only things that grow in the tundra are **mosses, lichens** and **grasses**. All of the plants in the tundra are small and grow low to the ground so that they can stay warm. They are very fragile plants. The tundra is a place where life is hard and short for all living things.

Edible plants. People have harvested wild plants for hundreds of years, using the roots, berries or leaves for nourishment or to spice up their meals. **Mint, peppermint, mustard, onion** and **wild carrot** all grow in Colorado and can be eaten. Another tasty treat is pine nuts harvested from the pine cones of the **piñon tree**.

One Colorado man used wild plants to create a multimillion dollar company. In 1969, Mo Siegel collected wild plants from the mountains near Boulder, dried the leaves, put them into tea bags and started what was to become the company Celestial Seasonings.

Wildflowers. Colorado's state flower is the **blue columbine**. It was chosen as the state flower in 1899 because of its colors. The blue was for the skies, the white for the snow and the yellow for the gold that had brought so many settlers here. It is against the law in Colorado to pick wild columbines.

Every spring the mountain meadows, prairies and plateaus of Colorado blossom with a wide variety of wildflowers. **Indian paintbrush, Johnny pop-up, forget-me-nots, buttercups** and **daisies** dot the countryside with blues, yellows, purples, reds, pinks and white.

NAME GAME

Directions. Just for the fun of it, find the name of a Colorado city or town to fit each definition below. These definitions are tricky! Ask your family or others to help you out. *Hints: Some of the answers are based on how a town is pronounced, not how it is spelled. Some items have more than one correct answer.*

1. The last name of a folk singer popular for his song about the Rocky Mountains *or* the last name of the person who played Gilligan on "Gilligan's Island."

_____

2. What you would surely use if you were brave enough to jump out of a plane!

_____

3. The color of Goldilocks' hair.

_____

4. Where the Flintstones live.

_____

5. The national bird of the United States.

_____

6. You probably get drinks of water from one of these at school.

_____

7. A comb's partner.

_____

8. A sweet-sounding town.

_____

9. A palace made of stone.

_____

10. A big rock.

_____

11. A white-barked tree with leaves that shiver and quake.

_____

12. Nothing at all.

_____

13. Name of Niles' brother on a popular TV show set in Seattle (now in re-runs).

_____

14. To separate.

_____

15. What Michelangelo carved his statues from.

_____

16. Opposite of "big ounce."

_____

17. You might see these berries at Christmas time.

_____

18. A partner for a mallard duck.

_____

19. A cone-bearing tree.

_____

20. The path of a doe.

_____

21. A kind of make-up sold door-to-door.

_____

22. What a farmer might have if he grew a crop of sweeping utensils.

_____

23. A really enormous pile of pennies.

_____

24. A boy's name.

_____

25. A girls' name.

_____

26. If you were really hungry, you might say, "It's time we were _____ "

27. Name of the queen of England.

_____

28. Another way to say, "The potato state jumps!"

_____

29. What you might get if you crossed a lemon and a lime.

_____

30. A car built out of stones.

_____

31. What a bride wears.

_____

32. A town full of guys with a short name.

_____

33. Name of a New York canal.

_____

34. Lead singer of the musical group "The Doors."

_____

35. Now *you* make up a definition!

_____

_____

_____

	C	**O**	**L**	**O**	**R**	**A**	**D**	**O**
Places in Colorado		*Ouray*						
Things related to sports and recreation		*oars*						
Things commonly put on a pizza		*olives*						
Animals & birds you might find in Colorado		*osprey*						
Things you might wear		*overshoes*						
You pick a category!								

DIRECTIONS: How many answers can you find to the puzzle, left? For each category listed along the side of the puzzle, see if you can think of an appropriate word that begins with the letter at the top of the column. Give yourself one point for each item you list.

Yes, you can list more than one item in a box, and it's okay if you can't find an answer for some boxes. Feel free to get help from reference books, the Internet, your family or other sources. To help you get started, some items have been filled in for you.

COLORADO IN THE PAST

Claims and Divisions of Colorado Lands

Colorado became a state in 1876. Colorado was the 38th state added to the United States of America. However, the area known as Colorado today was not always named "Colorado." The maps, right, show some of Colorado's history:

How many different countries have claimed parts of Colorado?_____

Name these countries. _____ _____

_____ _____

How many other states have claimed parts of Colorado? _____

What was Colorado Territory first named? _____

Who do you suppose it was named after? _____

Did You Know?

It wasn't until 1920 that women won the right to vote all across the United States. Colorado, however, was ahead of the times. In a statewide ballot held in 1893, voters gave the right to vote to all women over the age of 21. Colorado became the first state in the country to include women in the voting population!

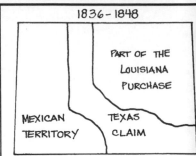

1540–1700 & 1763–1800

SPANISH CLAIM

(ENGLAND CLAIMED PARTS OF COLORADO, 1609–1763)

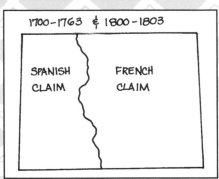

1700–1763 & 1800–1803

SPANISH CLAIM   FRENCH CLAIM

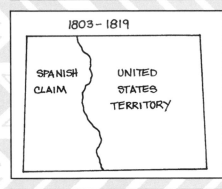

1803–1819

SPANISH CLAIM   UNITED STATES TERRITORY

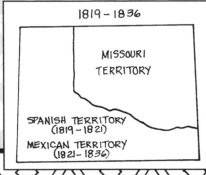

1819–1836

MISSOURI TERRITORY

SPANISH TERRITORY (1819–1821)
MEXICAN TERRITORY (1821–1836)

1836–1848

PART OF THE LOUISIANA PURCHASE

MEXICAN TERRITORY   TEXAS CLAIM

1850–1854

UTAH TERRITORY 1849–1850   UNITED STATES TERRITORY (UNORGANIZED)

NEW MEXICO TERRITORY

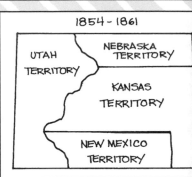

1854–1861

UTAH TERRITORY   NEBRASKA TERRITORY

KANSAS TERRITORY

NEW MEXICO TERRITORY

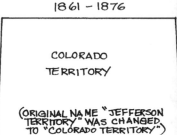

1861–1876

COLORADO TERRITORY

(ORIGINAL NAME "JEFFERSON TERRITORY" WAS CHANGED TO "COLORADO TERRITORY")

TRAILS

In the 19th century, the Native Americans who lived in the Colorado area established trails across the mountains and the plains. They formed the trails as they moved from summer camps to winter camps and as they followed the seasons in search of food. The trails generally stayed close to rivers in open areas. They also followed the shortest, easiest paths over the mountains.

When Spanish and English-speaking settlers arrived, they used these same trails to get where they needed to go. As Colorado became more and more settled in the 20th century, the trails were used to transport goods and products. They developed from dirt paths to gravel roads and, finally, to paved highways.

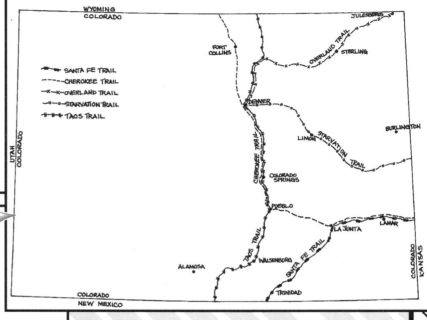

Look at the trails on the map, right.

- The Santa Fe Trail was one of the earliest and most important trails in Colorado. Color it red on the map.
- The Overland Trail carried more people than the Oregon or California trails. Color it brown.
- The Taos Trail was used as a short-cut for traders coming out of New Mexico and into Colorado when they wanted to get their products to the gold fields quickly. Color it green.
- Cherokee Indians used the Cherokee Trail on their way to the gold fields. Color it blue.
- The Starvation Trail was a short-cut for miners trying to get to the gold fields before anybody else. Color it yellow.

Look at the map of roads and highways, right.

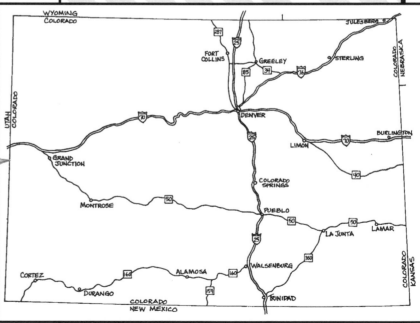

- What roads follow the Santa Fe Trail today? _____
- What roads follow the Overland Trail today? _____
- What roads follow the Taos Trail today? _____
- What roads follow the Cherokee Trail today? _____
- What roads follow the Starvation Trail today? _____

IMMIGRANTS & SETTLERS

Native Americans. The first people in the state who left evidence of themselves were the ancestral Puebloans, who lived in southwest Colorado. These cliff dwellers mysteriously disappeared around 1300 A.D.

Nomadic Native Americans moved in and out of Colorado for centuries. The Utes hunted deer and elk in the mountains. Members of the Cheyenne, Arapaho, Kiowa, Comanche and Apache tribes all lived and hunted on the Great Plains at various times between 1500 and 1880.

Japanese. Japanese immigrants arrived in Colorado in the early 1900s. They worked in the coal mines of southern Colorado, for the railroads, and in the sugar beet fields of the Arkansas and South Platte River valleys. Their numbers increased to over 20,000 by 1910.

During World War II, nearly 7,500 Japanese Americans from the West Coast were imprisoned in a camp called Amache, located east of Lamar. They had done nothing wrong, but some people in the United States were afraid that Japanese Americans would not be loyal during the war. Some of the Japanese Americans who were forced to come to Colorado decided to stay and make their homes here after the war.

The Spanish. Spanish soldiers and missionaries journeyed into Colorado beginning in 1541 with the expedition led by Francisco Coronado. They did not settle here then, but they explored much of the state and named many of the rivers and mountain ranges.

Farmers and cowboys. In 1862, the U.S. Congress passed the Homestead Act. It allowed people to claim 160 acres of land if they "proved" up on it within five years. This meant that they had to improve the land by planting and harvesting a crop and building a house, barn and corrals. Farmers came from all over the world to homestead land in Colorado between 1870 and 1920.

Cowboys who drove cattle along the Goodnight-Loving Trail through Colorado liked what they saw and decided to stay, too. The crop they raised was beef.

Germans from Russia. Long ago, Catherine the Great of Russia promised German farmers that they could keep their German language and customs if they would come to Russia and farm on the Russian frontier. About a hundred years ago, Czar Alexander II went back on Catherine's promise. Many Germans from Russia left and came to Colorado. They brought sturdy wheat seeds and started the planting of winter wheat. They also brought the knowledge and experience of sugar beet farming and helped make sugar beets a major Colorado crop.

Mexicans. Citizens of Mexico attempted to settle the San Luis Valley as early as 1833, but attacks from Native Americans drove them many times. Finally, in Mexican families from established the first per nent settlement in Col at San Luis.

A second wave of M immigrants came almos years later to help win Bracero program, an ag the United States and M Mexican laborers to wo jobs during the war, wh shortage of farm worke ended, many of the Me made their homes in C

Black Americans. Bla to Colorado in large nu War, looking for land, nities. In Colorado, the in greater numbers and blacks in any other state

Chinese. The first Asian people to come to Colorado were the Chinese, who came in the 1870s. After helping to build the western half of the transcontinental railroad, many Chinese people came to the bustling gold and silver mining camps in Leadville, Gregory Gulch, and Silverton. There was such discrimination against them, however, that by 1920 there were fewer than 300 Chinese people left in Colorado.

People with health problems. Starting in the 1870s, some people came to Colorado for health reasons. People who suffered from asthma and tuberculosis came to our state because of its dry, mild climate and many hot springs.

Soldiers. In the early 1940s, many U.S. citizens came to Colorado to train at military bases during World War II. After the war, many returned to Colorado to build homes and start families.

One of the groups that trained here was the 10th Mountain Division of the United States Army. The soldiers trained near Leadville and learned to fight on skis and snowshoes so they could defeat Hitler's German army in the European mountains. Many of these soldiers later returned to Colorado and helped develop Colorado's ski industry.

E ach one of us is connected to the past through our ancestors. Some of us know a lot about our ancestors, and some of us do not. Write about *one* of the subjects below. (You may want to ask your parents, grandparents or other relatives for help.)

1. **How you came to be in Colorado.** When, how and why did you and/or your family come to Colorado? Was it recently? Was it a long time ago? Where did your family come from? Which part of Colorado did your family settle in? Explain.

2. **Your ancestors.** Write about your ancestors. Did they immigrate to the United States? Were they Native Americans? What did they do to earn a living? Where did they live? What else do you know about them? What makes you proud of them?

3. **A story about a certain ancestor.** Tell a story about one of your ancestors. Has a story about one of them been passed down from generation to generation in your family? Can your grandmother tell you a story about *her* grandmother? Is there a story connected to a family recipe, a quilt, or a piece of furniture, for example? Write about what you discover.

_____

_____

_____

_____

_____

_____

_____

_____

FAMOUS COLORADANS

Many fascinating people have lived in Colorado. Look over the list below and choose someone who sounds interesting to you. (You may also choose someone not on this list. There are *many* famous Coloradans!) Find out more about the person you have chosen, using the library, your local museum, the Internet, interviews with people who have known the person, or other sources. Create a profile of the person on page 37.

Felipe and Dolores Baca. Ranchers who were among the founders of Trinidad.

Casimiro Barela. State Senator and early Hispanic leader.

Jim Beckwourth. Former slave who came west and became a mountain man and scout.

William and Charles Bent. Fur traders who founded the Bent's Old Fort trading post.

Black Kettle. Cheyenne chief who tried to keep peace with settlers.

Charles Boettcher. Philanthropist and founder of the Great Western Sugar Company.

Helen Bonfils. Philanthropist and publisher of the *Denver Post*.

"Aunt" Clara Brown. Former slave who became a philanthropist.

Molly Brown. Denverite who survived the sinking of the *Titanic*.

William Byers. Founder of the *Rocky Mountain News*.

Ben Nighthorse Campbell. Olympic athlete, U.S. Representative and U.S. Senator.

Scott Carpenter. One of the original Mercury program astronauts.

"Kit" Carson. Trapper, frontiersman, Indian agent and guide.

"Buffalo Bill" Cody. Star of "Buffalo Bill's Wild West" show.

Jack Dempsey. American world heavyweight boxing champion.

John Denver. Singer, songwriter and actor.

Mamie Dowd Eisenhower. Former first lady of the United States.

Douglas Fairbanks. Famous silent screen actor.

Barney Ford. Businessman and civil rights leader in early Colorado history.

Bruce Ford. Pro rodeo star.

Dr. Justina Ford. Physician who helped Denver's sick and needy.

Rudolfo "Corky" Gonzales. Civil rights leader.

Zane Grey. Author of many Western novels.

Emily Griffith. Founder of the Emily Griffith Opportunity School in 1916.

Ruth Handley. Inventor of the Barbie Doll in 1959.

Bill Hosakawa. World War II journalist and author.

Helen Hunt Jackson. 19th century author and activist for Native American rights.

O.T. Jackson. Founder of the black colony of Dearfield.

Edwin C. Johnson. Colorado's only three-time governor.

William "Billy" Kidd. Olympic ski champion.

Louis L'Amour. Author of numerous Western novels.

James Michener. Author of *Centennial* and other books.

Glenn Miller. Popular swing band leader during the 1930s and 1940s.

Enos Mills. Naturalist who helped create Rocky Mountain National Park.

Chief Ouray. Leader of the Southern Ute Indian tribe in the mid 1800s.

David Packard. Engineer who co-founded Hewlett-Packard.

Federico Peña. Former U.S. Secretary of Transportation.

Josephine Roche. Coal mine owner, social reformer and Denver's first female police officer.

Damon Runyon. Author of many plays, including the Broadway hit *Guys and Dolls*.

Florence Sabin. First female member of the National Academy of Sciences.

Patricia Schroeder. The longest serving woman in the U.S. House of Representatives.

F.O. Stanley. Co-inventor of the Stanley Steamer automobile.

Thomas Sutherland. Professor held hostage in Lebanon.

Lowell Thomas. Journalist known for his travels around the world.

Dalton Trumbo. Oscar-winning author and screenwriter.

Byron White. Pro-football player who became a U.S. Supreme Court Justice.

Paul Whiteman. Leader of the Paul Whiteman Orchestra, a popular band in the 1920s.

PROFILE
OF

_____

Name

_____

Years of birth and death

What did the person you have chosen accomplish in his or her life? What is the person noted for? Explain.

_____
_____
_____
_____
_____

In the space above, draw a picture of the person you have chosen. Or make a photocopy of a photograph to paste in the space.

What is the most interesting thing you found out about this person? Explain.

_____
_____
_____
_____

NATIONAL PARKS & MONUMENTS

Colorado has four national parks and five national monuments. Find out about them by using tourist brochures, the Internet, reference books, maps and people you know.

Match the descriptions on the left with the parks and monuments on the right. Write the number of each description below the correct name. There will be more than one answer for each park. Items #1 and #2 have been completed for you, as examples.

1. The name is a Ute word for "deserted valley."
2. Tourists drive on Trail Ridge Road to see the sights here.
3. It looks like a giant crack in the earth.
4. The name means "green table" in Spanish.
5. You can see fossilized brontosaurus here.
6. Contains the ruins of many towers.
7. You can go "sand boarding" here.
8. Located west of Pikes Peak.
9. Preserves plants and animals from over 35 million years ago.
10. Located on Sleeping Ute Mountain.
11. This new park was called a monument until December, 2000.
12. Located in Utah and the southwest corner of Colorado.
13. This area has more than 100 peaks over 10,000 feet high.
14. You might stay in Montrose if you visit.
15. The location of a 12 story stone "apartment building."
16. The Continental Divide runs through it.

17. Includes over 20,000 acres of deep canyons and huge natural rock towers.
18. This site has 15-20 foot high mounds that preserve an unexcavated prehistoric village.
19. Located in Utah and the northwest corner of Colorado.
20. The Yampa River and the Green River run through this area.
21. Visitors to this place often stay in Estes Park.
22. You can see huge, petrified redwood trees here.
23. Has one of the world's largest collections of dinosaur bones.
24. Visitors often stay in Grand Junction.
25. The site of rock formations called Independence Monument and Pipe Organs.
26. There are over 1000 archaeological sites here.
27. Contains a narrow, rugged canyon that is very steep and over 2000 feet deep in some places.
28. An area that was occupied by a large farming culture from about 500 B.C. until 1300 A.D. (*This description fits two places!*)

Rocky Mountain National Park:
2, _____

Mesa Verde National Park:
_____

Black Canyon of the Gunnison National Park:
_____

Great Sand Dunes National Park:
_____

Dinosaur National Monument:
_____

Hovenweep National Monument:
1, _____

Florissant Fossil Beds National Monument:
_____

Colorado National Monument:
_____

Yucca House National Monument:
_____

Choose one of the parks or monuments listed above. Using books, pamphlets or other sources, find out more about the park or monument. Then summarize one fact or interesting piece of information, below. _____
_____
_____
_____
_____

RURAL & URBAN COLORADO

People who live in cities or towns live in *urban* areas. People who live in the country live in *rural* areas. People who grow crops, raise livestock and produce food are also called *rural*. How would you define yourself — as *rural* or *urban*? Why?

_____

_____

_____

_____

Population density. Population density refers to the average number of people per square mile living in an area. When there are many people per square mile, an area is considered urban. When there are few people per square mile, an area is considered rural.

The population density of each of six Colorado counties is listed below. Suppose that a population density of 100 or more people per square mile indicates that a county is urban. Label each of the counties as "urban" or "rural," based on its population density:

_____ **Dolores County.** 1.4 people per square mile

_____ **Denver County.** 3,050 people per square mile

_____ **Eagle County.** 13 people per square mile

_____ **Crowley County.** 5 people per square mile

_____ **Boulder County.** 303 people per square mile

_____ **Jefferson County.** 568 people per square mile

Industries of Colorado

Look at the two pie charts on this page. They show how various industries have contributed to Colorado's economy. One chart is for the year 1929, and the other is for the year 2000.

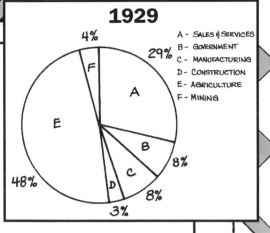

1929

A – SALES & SERVICES
B – GOVERNMENT
C – MANUFACTURING
D – CONSTRUCTION
E – AGRICULTURE
F – MINING

- Which industry contributed the most to Colorado's economy in 1929? _____

- Which industry contributed the most in 2000? _____

- What happened to construction between 1929 and 2000?

  _____

Sales and services jobs occur more often in urban areas, while agricultural jobs occur more often in rural areas.

- Was Colorado more urban or more rural in 1929? How do you know?

  _____

  _____

  _____

- Was Colorado more urban or more rural in 2000? How do you know?

  _____

  _____

  _____

  _____

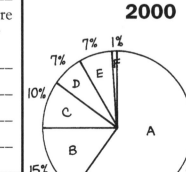

2000

A – SALES & SERVICES
B – GOVERNMENT
C – MANUFACTURING
D – CONSTRUCTION
E – AGRICULTURE
F – MINING

Rural Colorado

Almost one-half (49%) of the land in Colorado is made up of farms and ranches. The people who live on the farms and ranches are involved in *agriculture*. Agriculture refers to producing crops and raising livestock.

Colorado farmers and ranchers produce crops and livestock that are used throughout the state, the nation and the world. Sometimes we don't think about the connection between a product we buy in the store and where it came from. Look at the following list of some of the animals raised in Colorado. Draw a line matching each animal with the items that we buy from a store, on the right.

Cattle

Sheep

Hogs

Chickens

bacon
blankets
yogurt
chicken nuggets
leather shoes
eggs
footballs
hand lotion with lanolin
ham
wool sweaters

See if you can think of six more items in your home that are produced from the animals above.

_____ _____

_____ _____

_____ _____

Colorado farmers raise many crops. Some of the most common ones are listed below, along with the counties that produce most (not all!) of these crops. Follow the instructions after each item, using the county map, right.

- Counties where winter or spring wheat is grown: *Weld, Logan, Sedgwick, Phillips, Yuma, Washington, Adams, Morgan, Arapahoe, Elbert, Larimer, Lincoln, Kit Carson, Cheyenne, Kiowa, Prowers, Conejos, Costilla, Saguache, Baca, Rio Grande.* Put a brown dot in each of these counties.

- Counties where corn is grown: *Weld, Morgan, Logan, Sedgwick, Phillips, Yuma, Washington, Cheyenne, Otero, Prowers, Baca.* Put a yellow dot in each of these counties.

- Counties where cantaloupes are grown: *Otero, Crowley, Delta.* Put an orange dot in each of these counties.

- Counties where sugar beets are grown: *Larimer, Weld, Morgan, Logan, Yuma.* Put a purple dot in each of these counties.

- Counties where potatoes are grown: *Rio Grande, Saguache, Costilla, Alamosa, Weld, Yuma.* Put a pink dot in each of these counties.

- Counties where peaches, pears, cherries or apples are grown: *Mesa* and *Delta*. Put a red dot in each of these counties.

- Counties where hay is grown: *Montezuma, La Plata, Montrose, Delta, Mesa, Garfield, Rio Blanco, Moffat, Routt, Jackson, Larimer, Weld, Logan, Morgan, Washington, Yuma, Kit Carson, Elbert, El Paso, Pueblo, Baca, Las Animas, Costilla, Alamosa, Saguache, Rio Grande, Conejos, Bent, Prowers.* Put a green dot in each of these counties.

1. Count the dots in each county. Using this number as your key, which county is the most agricultural? _____

2. Look at the counties along the Continental Divide. What conclusion can you make about farming in this area? _____

_____

3. In the counties that contain only green dots for "hay," which would you expect to see — more ranches or more farms?_____ Why?_____

_____

4. Find the county where you live. Shade it light green. Are there crops grown in your county? If so, which ones? _____

MORE RURAL & URBAN

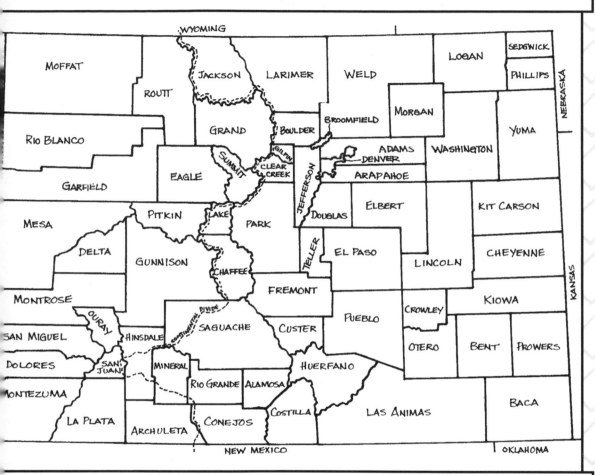

Urban Colorado

1. In order from largest to smallest, the largest urban areas in Colorado are:

- Denver metropolitan area
- Colorado Springs
- Fort Collins
- Pueblo
- Boulder
- Greeley
- Longmont
- Loveland
- Grand Junction

Mark these cities on the Colorado map, left, and draw a large rectangle around those east of the Continental Divide. This area is called the "Front Range Corridor." Experts say that within 20 years this entire rectangle will be one big urban area.

2. Transportation plays a very big role in the location of towns and cities. Many cities grow up where a trail crosses a river, where two trails meet, where two rivers meet, or at the entrance of a canyon that leads to the mountains. Choose two of Colorado's cities. Study a map. Why do you think they might have grown up where they are?

_____

_____

_____

_____

_____

_____

ter you have
ompleted the
ctions on page
eate your own map key for the
bove. The map key should
e all the different colored
own on the map and the
hey represent.

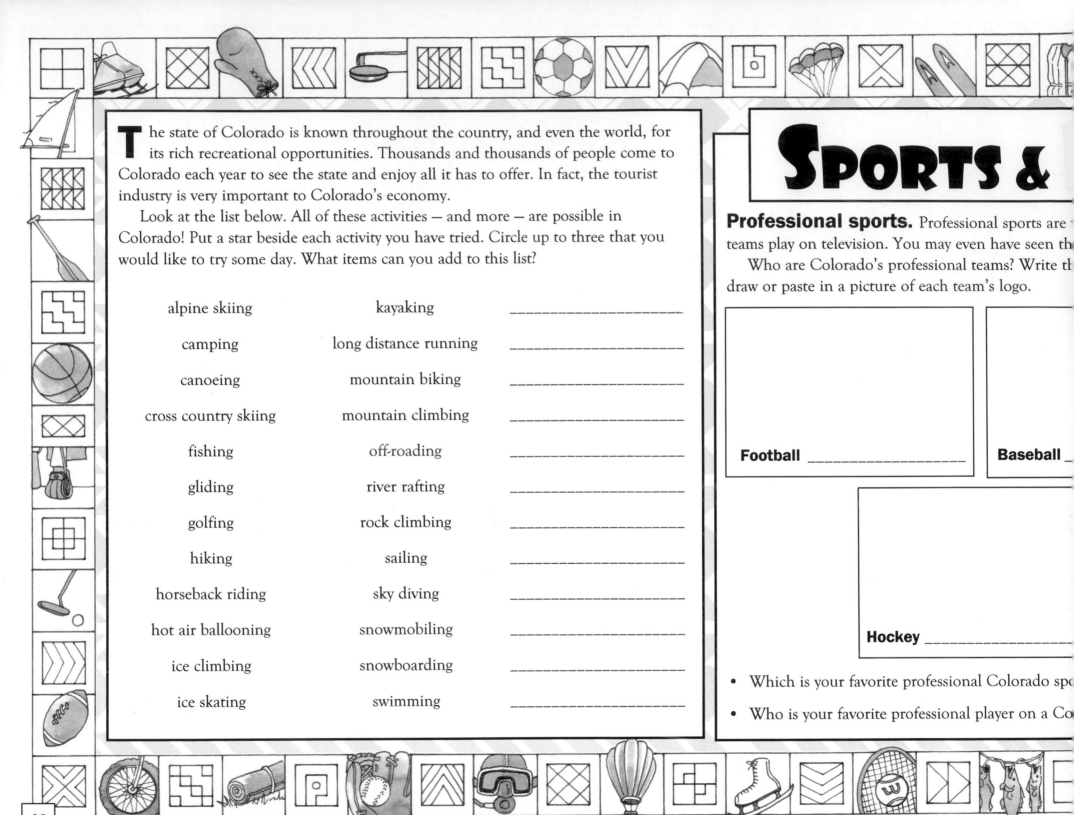

The state of Colorado is known throughout the country, and even the world, for its rich recreational opportunities. Thousands and thousands of people come to Colorado each year to see the state and enjoy all it has to offer. In fact, the tourist industry is very important to Colorado's economy.

Look at the list below. All of these activities — and more — are possible in Colorado! Put a star beside each activity you have tried. Circle up to three that you would like to try some day. What items can you add to this list?

alpine skiing	kayaking	_____
camping	long distance running	_____
canoeing	mountain biking	_____
cross country skiing	mountain climbing	_____
fishing	off-roading	_____
gliding	river rafting	_____
golfing	rock climbing	_____
hiking	sailing	_____
horseback riding	sky diving	_____
hot air ballooning	snowmobiling	_____
ice climbing	snowboarding	_____
ice skating	swimming	_____

SPORTS &

Professional sports. Professional sports are
teams play on television. You may even have seen th
Who are Colorado's professional teams? Write th
draw or paste in a picture of each team's logo.

Football _____

Baseball _

Hockey _____

- Which is your favorite professional Colorado sp
- Who is your favorite professional player on a Co

CREATION

...r in Colorado. You have probably seen Colorado
...person.

...each team in the correct space below. Then either

Basketball _____

...cer _____

_____

Olympic sports.
Because of Colorado's high elevation, many athletes who depend on endurance training to improve their performance come to Colorado.

- The U.S. Olympic Training Center in Colorado Springs is one of three centers where athletes train for U.S. Olympic teams. They practice swimming, skating, gymnastics, volleyball, basketball, boxing, judo and 38 other sports.
- Many marathon runners and bicyclists train in Boulder.
- Mountain ski areas such as Vail and Steamboat Springs provide Olympic skiers and jumpers the opportunity to improve their skills.

The team from Joes.
In the 1920s, a group of Colorado boys proved how important it is to practice and train for a sport, and then practice and train some more.

The boys lived in the town of Joes, which then had a population of 91 people. The boys loved basketball. They drew a court in the hard packed dirt of their school playground and stuck two poles in the ground. On the poles they nailed empty vinegar barrels with the bottoms punched out. Then they began to play basketball. By the time they were in high school, they had practiced together so long and so hard that they were a great team.

The boys from Joes beat all the other high school teams in Colorado in 1929, winning the state basketball championship. Then they went to the national high school basketball finals in Chicago, where each of the 48 state champions participated in a tournament. The team from Joes beat each team it played and reached the semifinals. The team came in third with a record of 41-2 for that year.

For the three cousins and their classmates who made up the team from Joes, lots and lots of practice turned out to be more important than either school size or equipment. Upside-down vinegar barrels and a dirt court were good enough for these Colorado champions!

ROAD TRIP

Imagine that you are going to take a road trip around Colorado to learn more about its interesting places, exciting history and beautiful landscapes. Plan your trip, following the directions below.

1. Decide on 10 places in the state that you wish to visit. Use the list at the right for suggestions. (You may also choose other places that are not listed. There are many wonderful places to go in Colorado.) Be sure to include the following in your 10 places:

- at least one place in the mountains
- at least one place on the plains
- at least one place on the Colorado Plateau
- at least one place in a big city
- at least one place in a rural area

2. Find your 10 places on a road map of Colorado. If you were driving, which highways and roads would you take?

3. An *itinerary* is an outline of a trip. It lists the places you will go, in the order you will visit them. List your itinerary on page 45.

4. Draw a postcard from one of the places you "visited." Use the box provided on the next page.

Bonus challenge: Use a road map to determine approximately how many miles you will drive on your trip. If you travel an average of 60 miles per hour, how many hours will you spend traveling?

Just a Few Places to Visit in Colorado

National Parks and Monuments. Black Canyon of the Gunnison N... Great Sand Dunes National Park, Mesa Verde National Park, Rocky M... National Park, Colorado National Monument, Dinosaur National Mo... rissant Fossil Beds National Monument, Hovenweep National Monum... House National Monument.

Denver/Boulder area. Molly Brown House Museum, Governor's... Colorado State Capitol, Denver Art Museum, Denver Botanic Gar... Mint, Denver Zoo, Denver Museum of Nature and Science, Hyland... World, Colorado History Museum, Denver Firefighters Museum, R... Amphitheater, Black American West Museum and Heritage Center... Grave and Museum, Colorado Railroad Museum, National Center... spheric Research, Mother Cabrini Shrine, Butterfly Pavilion and In...

Colorado Springs area. Cheyenne Mountain Zoo, Garden of the... Falls, U.S. Air Force Academy, Cave of the Winds, Pikes Peak, Pro... of Fame and Museum of the American Cowboy, World Figure Ska... and Hall of Fame, Western Museum of Mining and Industry.

Other. Buena Vista: St. Elmo Ghost Town. **Burlington:** Kit Carso... Carousel. **Canyon City:** Royal Gorge. **Central City:** Central City Op... **Chivington:** Sand Creek Massacre Monument. **Cortez:** Four Corne... **Crested Butte:** Mountain Bike Hall of Fame. **Dolores:** Anasazi Heri... **Delta:** Fort Uncompahgre Living History Museum. **Durango:** Dura... ton Narrow Gauge Railroad. **Glenwood Springs:** Doc Holliday's Gr... Hot Springs Pool. **Greeley:** Centennial Village. **Idaho Springs:** St. M... Argo Gold Mine. **La Junta:** Bent's Old Fort National Historic Site... National Mining Hall of Fame and Museum, Tabor Opera House. ... Dempsey Museum. **Montrose:** Ute Indian Museum. **Ouray-Silverto...** Dollar Highway. **Pueblo:** Colorado Fuel and Iron Plant, El Pueblo ... **Luis:** Shrine of the Stations of the Cross. **Steamboat Springs:** Straw... Springs. **Vail:** Colorado Ski Museum-Hall of Fame. **Salida:** Salida H...

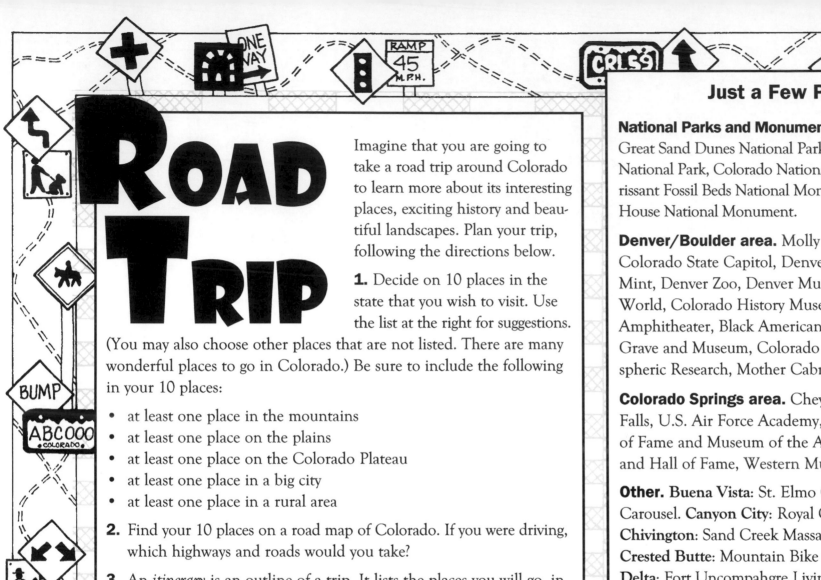

Trip Itinerary

1. _____

2. _____

3. _____

4. _____

5. _____

6. _____

7. _____

8. _____

9. _____

10. _____

Draw your postcard here.

BONUS CHALLENGE

TOTAL TRIP MILEAGE _____

TOTAL HOURS OF TRAVELING TIME _____

COLO
H
IN THE
M

Though you m
it, history is b
of the year. Event
lines today will ap
or fifty years from

Using current
state or natic
think may be imp
these headlines in
left.

ADO
TORY
KING

p to think about
e every single day
ole making head-
story books forty

s, collect local,
nes that you
uture years. Paste
on the right and

A to Z

Directions. Remember those alphabet books you used to read when you were small? Imagine you are making an alphabet book just for Colorado. Think of at least one Colorado item for each letter of the alphabet. For example, you might consider names of people, places, events, animals or plants. Write your alphabet items beside the letters, below.

Here are some examples to get you started:

Aspen

Brown, Molly

Colorado Avalanche

A

B

C

D

E

F

G

H

I

J

K

L

M

N

O

P

Q

R

S

T

U

V

W

X

Y

Z